NORFOLK & W
DIESEL'S LAST CONQUEST

BY

WILLIAM E. WARDEN

T L C
PUBLISHING

ROUTE 4, BOX 154
LYNCHBURG, VIRGINIA 24503

i

FRONT COVER ILLUSTRATION: An original painting, done for this book by Andrew Harmantas, represents a typical scene during N&W's steam-diesel transition years, as a Y-6b 2-8-8-2 articulated is overtaken by The Pocahontas with the new tuscan red GP-9s in the lead, somewhere between Bluefield and Williamson, West Virginia.

Library of Congress Catalogue Number: 91-66374
ISBN Number: 0-9622003-6-0

Typography & Layout
by
Thomas W. Dixon, Jr. & Carolyn B. Dixon

First Printing, 1991
Second Printing, 1995
Third Printing, 1996

Printing by
Walsworth Publishing Company
306 North Kansas Avenue
Marceline, Missouri 64658

INTRODUCTION

That the Norfolk & Western Railway was the last holdout of steam—in 1954 every freight and passenger train, every yard movement, was powered by the force of expanding vaporized water on piston surfaces—can not be questioned. Nor can the fact that by 1960, after what the May 1960 issue of Trains characterized as "N&W's...forced-draft dieselization program," N&W train movements were 100 percent behind diesels.

This book is not about diesels as such—others have detailed the specifications and abilities of RS-3s and 11s, T-6 switchers, and GP-9s and 18s down to the last rivet—but rather how the N&W's dieselization was accomplished and why it was accomplished when it was. Norfolk & Western Train Watchers in the mid-1950s were understandably dismayed by watching their pet 2-8-8-2s, 2-6-6-4s, 4-8-4s, and 0-8-0s disappear like Winter snows on a warm Spring day and they deserve a concise and balanced rationale for the N&W abandoning steam. The author has attempted within these pages to provide that rationale.

For a book of this size to record the whole story of dieselization, certain constraints have been applied. Consequently, the story being told is of all diesels, whether owned, borrowed, or just passing through that ran on N&W tracks up to the time of the final GP-18 delivery, at which point, for all intents and purposes, the Railway's dieselization was complete. A brief nod to newer diesels is also given, however. Former Virginian Railway diesels are omitted as they have been treated adequately in other books, most notably in H. Reid's *The Virginian Railway*, and because the Virginian's diesels seldom saw service on post-1959 N&W tracks.

With respect to dieselization, the Railway continued the policy it had long followed with its justly-famous steam locomotives of settling on a few standard designs that could meet the requirements of almost every division.

Interestingly, N&W dieselization coincided with the transition of diesels from high-powered specialty items that operated in more-or-less fixed combinations—EMD's E- and F- class diesels where the "B" units were virtually useless unless attached to one or more "A" units, for example—to building-block "units" that could be hooked together in any manner considered suitable, and in any number the road foreman of engines deemed appropriate to get a train of "X" tons over a ruling grade of "Y" percent in "Z" minutes. And the only features that might differentiate passenger and freight units were traction motor gear ratios and—sometimes—paint scheme.

If a railroad book may be said to have a hero and a villain, this one has President R. H. ("Race Horse") Smith who agonized over acquisition of the first diesels, and Stuart T. Saunders who presided over the final dismantling of the N&W's steam fleet. Which man fills which role will be left up to the reader to decide.

So sit back and relax now while we see how a railroad long famous for its devotion to "Super Power" steam reluctantly bit the bullet of dieseldom and switched from the products of its own Roanoke Shops to those of Schenectady and LaGrange.

Acknowledgments

Production of this book was much more than simply the efforts of author and publisher. I'd like to thank the following for their kind and gracious help, without which this book could never have come to be:

Howard W. Ameling, William R. Baumgardner, Jr., Art Bixby, Ed Crist, H. H. Harwood, Jr., Gene Huddleston, Steve Patterson, C. E. Pond, M. D. McCarter, Ken Miller, C. Grattan Price, Jr., E. A. Honeycutt, Paul W. Prescott, H. Reid, Jim Shaughnessy, Joe Schmitz, Curt Tillotson, Jr., Virginia Polytechnic Institute & State University (photos from this institution are credited "N&W, VPI&SU," indicating that they are from the N&W Photographic Collection held there), and Aubrey Wiley.

And a special thanks goes to the late Ben B. Dulaney, N&W Manager of News and Community Services, excellent friend, guide, and mentor, and the first person who thought I could reduce to print the story of N&W's dieselization.

William E. Warden
July 12, 1991

THE DIESELS ARRIVE

Never, thought hogger Bill Fortune, had he seen so many officials gathered around a freight train in the West Roanoke Yard as there were on that warm, sunny, February 14th morning in 1956.

Why, there was Clarence Pond (the N&W's Motive Power Superintendent and as knowledgeable a steam man as any railroad ever employed), Chief Mechanical Inspector Hobart Scott, and even President R. H. "Race Horse" Smith!

Small wonder. Instead of the usual painting Y-class 2-8-8-2 on the point of the 196-car, 4550-ton westbound drag, were the N&W's Dynamometer Car and four shiny burbling Alco RS-3 diesel units, Nos. 92, 93, 94 and 95, the first diesels with N&W logos that Bill or almost anyone else in West Roanoke had seen. The N&W had taken delivery of them only a couple of weeks earlier and when testing was completed, they'd join four sister RS-3s that had been operating on the Lynchburg-Durham line since October 1955.

The N&W had just placed an order for 75 Alco and General Motors diesel units and there had been rumors around Roanoke that management would soon stage tests to see how these new-fangled machines would operate in mountainous territory. Only yesterday, Bill Fortune had received word that he just might be the engineer on the first test train and now all the speculation had come true. This was quite an honor for a young fellow who had made his first trip in charge of the right-hand side of a locomotive cab just seven years earlier.

Fortune was a dedicated steam man but, after comparing watches with conductor L. J. Payne, he felt a surge of excitement as he climbed into the cab of lead diesel, No. 92.

In No. 92's cab was a trio of Alco field engineers who hovered nervously over Fortune, while offering instructions. The Alco's controls, however, resembled those of the N&W's star-crossed steam turbine *Jawn Henry*, which Fortune had operated several times in the past. He had no trouble easing the diesel freight out of Roanoke and onto the Radford Division.

The Alcos hammered their way up Christiansburg Hill at a minimum speed of 11 miles per hour. Then, just before the Hill was crested, an air hose burst on the fifth car from the front end and it appeared the test run was off to an inauspicious start. But 35 minutes later, after some hasty repairs, the train was on its way.

A light rain greeted the train after passing Narrows. The rain caused some wheel slipping on the grade east of Bluefield and speed was reduced to a crawl. The diesels never lost traction completely, however, and Fortune had his train past Bluefield passenger station at 3:10 p.m., less than six hours after leaving Roanoke.

At Bluefield, the train stopped only long enough to change crews, then continued on to Iaeger, arriving there at 6:14 p.m. That night, the diesels were coupled to a 17,000-ton eastbound train at Iaeger's Auville yard. Then, assisted by Y-6b class 2-8-8-2 No. 2185, they went charging out of Iaeger for Bluefield.

When the Alco's tapes came off the Dynamometer Car recorders and were put together with similar tapes made from test runs on the first General Motors GP-9's delivered in October 1955, the evidence was rather conclusive. The diesels had gotten over the road faster and cheaper than just about any steam locomotive had done with comparable tonnage. The Norfolk & Western Railway had at last entered—reluctantly it seemed—the diesel age. And engineer Fortune had opened the door wide.

By rights, the N&W should, at this point, have entered a crash program of dieselization. Yet as the railroad industry and train watchers alike wondered, the N&W took almost four more years to retire all its steamers. What was the reason for this strange and anachronistic allegiance to steam at a time when almost every other Class I railroad in the United States was 100 percent dependent upon internal combustion-driven motive power?

And although this is a book about N&W diesels, you gentle reader, are perfectly justified in questioning why the steamers hung on so long. The question is particularly pertinent when you consider that Rudolph Diesel's machine had on several occasions powered the N&W freights and varnish before appearing on the Lynchburg-Durham line.

(In fact the first diesel units actually appeared on the N&W back in 1938, yes 1938, when three EMC [not EMD] 2,000 horsepower units were forwarded dead from Clare Yard to Petersburg in Train No. 84. They had been ordered by the Seaboard Air Line to power its recently dieselized *Orange Blossom Special*.)

Snarling Southern Railway E-8s and FP-7s had hauled the joint Southern-N&W passenger train through between Lynchburg and Bristol during the 1950 coal miners' strike. It is said that when the first diesel-powered passenger train—No. 45, the *Tennessean*—arrived in Roanoke, there was a crowd out just to see it.

N&W management reviewed the Southern's impressive figures for fuel economy and maintenance costs over this stretch of mountainous track, gave a polite corporate yawn, and resumed operating its enormously efficient J-class 4-8-4s on the joint varnish as soon as the strike was over. Then in September 1952, in what most steam aficionados considered an act of heresy, the N&W permitted General Motors to try out 6,000 horsepower F-7 class diesel No. 459, scheduled for delivery to the Union Pacific, on the Pocahontas and Scioto Divisions. The 459 had previously made a shakedown run on the Chicago and Northwestern.

For nearly three weeks the 4-unit diesel muscled 16,000-ton coal drags over the Scioto Division between

Williamson and Portsmouth, Ohio, at average speeds of better that 30 miles per hour. Similar tests were subsequently run on the Pocahontas Division between Williamson and Bluefield and 459 hauled 10,000 tons from Williamson to Farm at an average of 23 miles per hour. Geared for a maximum speed of 65 miles per hour, No. 459 performed well if not spectacularly. On one run the diesel managed to shave 28 minutes off the Williamson-Bluefield schedule of time freight No. 86. Later, replacing a Y-6b 2-8-8-2 on the rear of a coal drag, it helped boost 8,300 tons over the grade from Farm to Bluefield. This was an increase of 1,700 tons over the rating of two Y-6b's on the same track. Indeed, 459's builders modestly suggested that helper service would be the ideal assignment for their F-7s.

However, when the GM salesmen whipped out their order books, they were met with a firm "no thank you." After all, there were those almost new steamers in the roundhouse, on-line coal was plentiful and cheap, and *Jawn Henry*, promising a renaissance of steam, was about to be outshopped, (actually, *Jawn* did deliver freight at a fuel cost lower than that of the F-7 demonstrator but his complex machinery problems and lower-than-expected thermal efficiency relegated him to retirement on the last day of 1957, well in advance of most other N&W steamers. (See page 11). Then too, N&W people from President Smith on down had an almost fanatical devotion to steam.

This devotion, probably more than any other factor explains why, even in 1956, the Railway was not about to give up its dependence on its traditional motive power.

But if N&W brass could delay dieselization they could not do so indefinitely. Even in 1956 there were forces economic, logistical, and human at work, that made steam's demise as sure as death and taxes. Some of these forces—difficulty in obtaining replacement parts, aging of those steamers that might have powered locals economically, etc.—have been discussed in other books. We will take a look at some of the other forces here shortly.

Smith's devotion to steam was not without a solid economic foundation at least at the time Bill Fortune was starting his memorable test run. While almost all other Class I roads had scrapped steam by the mid-1950's, the 100 percent steam-driven N&W was posting operating ratios in the low 70's and high 60's and was constantly among the five most profitable railroads in the country.

Then in 1954, came the little-noticed first break with steam.

In November of that year, the N&W pur-

chased the 56-mile 100 percent dieselized Chesapeake Western, located in Virginia's lush Shenandoah Valley. But shucks, the CW was run as a semi-independent subsidiary—it even occupied its own spot in the *Official Guide* (with R. H. Smith listed as its president)—and its motive power strayed no further on to N&W track than a connecting siding at Elkton, where it dropped off turkeys (Harrisonburg, twenty-five miles to the west billed itself as the "Turkey Capital of the World") and picked up a few coal cars. Technically at least, the N&W owned no diesels but rather rostered 444 steam locomotives as 1954 drew to a close.

But in 1955, the break with 100 percent steam became a clean one.

An unpublicized order was quietly placed for eight

One of the original RS-3s on the property, No. 307, is engaged in some switching in the Bellevue, Ohio, yards. The RS-3s with their low hoods were easily distinguished from their younger sisters, the RS-11s. Note the Nickel Plate caboose. The merger of the Nickel Plate, Wabash, et al, is not yet a year in the past and the N&W's car shops hadn't gotten around to the low priority job of repainting a perfectly good caboose. Photographed September, 1965.

Alco RS-3 diesels, including the four on which engineer Fortune made his test run. They were to be used on the lightly-trafficked Durham District, said the N&W's brief press notices, to release badly needed steam power—actually a few elderly Z-class 2-6-6-2s and K-1 class 4-8-2s — for service on the main line. When questioned, which was inevitable, President Smith was quick to point out that , "This does not mean that we have changed our view that our modern roller-bearing coal-burning steam locomotives can handle the major part of our traffic economically...." Other railroad presidents had made similar statements over the years so Smith's pronouncement was greeted with some skepticism.

Interestingly enough, these eight units, all built in late 1955 and early 1956, were the only RS-3s the road ever bought. Almost as soon as the -3s were delivered, the N&W began ordering the more powerful—1,800 vs 1,600 horsepower—Alco RS-11s until by mid-1961 it had

**N&W President
R. H. Smith**

acquired 94 of them. The RS-3s were ultimately numbered 300-307 and the -11s 308-406.

Dieselization might have stalled at Durham—with perhaps a few additional growlers to power local freights and mixed trains—for Lord knows how long. But those problems of aging steamers and a shortage of spare parts that couldn't be fabricated in house were beginning to be felt. Then there was an economic fact of life nobody could have foreseen earlier.

Coal traffic was still the lifeblood of the Norfolk & Western. The majority of its coal traffic—and consequently the majority of all freight traffic in the early 1950s moved westward from Williamson in 11,000 ton trains over gentle grades to Columbus. From there, it was shipped north to Great Lakes Ports and Midwest steel mills.

But suddenly the industrial plant of postwar Europe was burgeoning and the demand for high-grade metallurgical coal across the Atlantic was growing apace.

The N&W aimed to get a share of this new coal market. This meant new, longer, and faster eastbound trains out of West Virginia. The trial and failure of *Jawn Henry* demonstrated that there would be no immediate breakthrough in steam efficiency and availability — already higher on the N&W than almost anywhere else. Hence these new coal trains would need more helper engines to blast up the slopes of the Alleghenies and Blue Ridge if they were going to make it with steam.

Just as Europe began clamoring for metallurgical coal, the market for steam coal in this country began dropping, as electrical utilities, heretofore among the N&W's best customers and almost entirely coal fed, were converting their power plants to gas, oil, and that just aborning atomic power. To guard against the decline of this particular demand, the Norfolk & Western needed to increase its merchandise traffic. Doing this also dictated the need for heavier and faster trains.

Could the Road grab a portion of this new coal market and increased merchandise hauling (all this with steam and helper districts) in competition with its dieselized Pocahontas Region neighbors? The question was pondered long and hard in Roanoke headquarters. No amount of soul searching or emotional attachment could change the answer.

N&W management opted for full-scale dieselization. In late 1955 the road ordered 25 Alco RS-11s for use primarily between Portsmouth and Cincinnati. Early in 1956, an order was placed for 33 EMD GP-9s and 17 RS-11s for use on the Shenandoah Division between Hagerstown and Roanoke. Remember, GP-9s and RS-11s represented state-of-the-art diesel engineering then.

The die was cast; there was no turning back. The N&W dieselized for reasons different from those of, say, the New Haven or Santa Fe, but the end result in terms of internal combustion domination was the same.

Once the decision was made there was no feeling of urgency to enforce it throughout the railroad, however.

When the General Motors GP-9s and Alco RS-11s began arriving in earnest in 1956 and 57—108 in the latter year alone, it was feasible to get as much economical use out of the remaining coal burners as possible by concentrating them on the mainline east of Williamson. Here were located most of the finest steam servicing facilities and fuel sources for these engines. Effectively, the available motive power needed for increased business on the main line was increased by this concentration also.

The Road's extremities—the Scioto and Shenandoah Divisions were dieselized first and at an unexpectedly fast rate. So rapid was this dieselization that while the first diesel-powered train, headed by GP-9 No. 735, appeared on the Shenandoah Division in January 1957, the last steamer, Waynesboro yard switcher, 4-8-0 No. 1119, departed for good the following month.

Putting geeps on the Shenandoah Division early on made good sense on several counts. First, local freight–of which the division had a considerable amount, previously hauled by a monster 2-8-8-2 could now be handled by a single diesel unit with considerable saving in fuel costs. Actually, diesels saved an average of 50 cents per 1,000 gross ton-miles on all Shenandoah freight in 1957. Second, steam engine servicing facilities were not up to the standards of the main line. Third, the Division, via a friendly connection with the Pennsy at Hagerstown, was the N&W's principal conduit for highly competitive merchandise freight headed for the Northeast. And fourth, steam coal destined for Northeastern utilities, particularly New York's Consolidated Edison, also interchanged with the Pennsy at Hagerstown.

This last count explains why the N&W began sending unitized coal trains out on the Shenandoah Division in August 1962. Tie four, maybe five, GP-9s to the front of 110-120 hoppers, use another four as helpers between Natural Bridge and Lofton, and you have the perfect motive power combination to get a unitized coal train over the road at maximum speed and with minimum fuel cost.

Number 10, shown at Lynchburg, was one of the original order of GP-9s delivered in October 1955. It was renumbered 710 in 1956 and the original number assigned to one of the first T-6 class switchers.

N&W, VPI&SU

4

Despite the complete dieselization of two of its divisions, by the end of 1957 better than 50% of the N&W's mainline tonnage east of Williamson and 95% of all passenger car miles still moved behind steam. And although the road then owned 168 diesels, 346 steamers were still on the roster. Both steam and diesel fans viewed these statistics with wonderment and speculated that perhaps the N&W had done all the dieselization it was going to do—at least in the foreseeable future.

The speculation might have proved correct had not Smith been succeeded as N&W President by Stuart T. Saunders in April 1958. Suddenly the N&W was no longer an operating man's railroad. Born in McDowell County, West Virginia, but raised within whistle sound of the N&W mainline in Bedford, Virginia, the Harvard Law School-educated Saunders may have possessed little technical knowledge of a steam locomotive's operation but he knew his way around a profit and loss statement as few railroad presidents before or since. Aesthetics and sentiment be damned!

No sooner did Saunders take office than he turned his attention to the matter of dieselization. At that point, the Road owned 198 diesel units and 262 steamers. In addition, 30 Pennsy GP-9s, numbered 7200-7229, leased the previous December when deliveries were slow, were on the property.

On June 25, 1958, Saunders announced that the Norfolk & Western Railway would be completely dieselized by the end of 1960 with but 60 steam locomotives held "for standby service."

Few executive decisions ever raised such a storm of criticism. Saunders was accused of lacking sentiment for steam (unquestionably true) and of being pressured by the Pennsy which then owned a controlling interest in the N&W (a charge never proven).

Viewed in retrospect, however, Saunders had no options.

Inflation was spiraling operating costs a faster rate than revenues. The cost of coal relative to oil had been increasing. Drastic fuel and manpower economies were necessary if the road was to remain profitable. Then too the bogey that had haunted the Motive Power Department for several years was growing at an alarming rate — steam locomotive replacement parts that couldn't be fabricated in the Roanoke Shops were becoming almost impossible to obtain at any cost.

One factor generally overlooked in the fulmination over Saunder's decision was that the sheer size of the N&W's newer

N&W, VPI&SU

**N&W President
Stuart T. Saunders**

H. H. Harwood, Jr.

Leased PRR GP-9s 7215, 7200, and 7229 on an empty train on Christiansburg Grade in June 1958.

steam locomotives would inevitably doom them. By 1958 there was considerable historical evidence that this was so. The last steamers on the Wabash had been a trio of Edwardian-era Moguls. The Pennsy was still operating K-4 class 4-6-2s in its North Jersey suburban service long after the duplex drives and decapods had been scrapped. And the last New York Central steam run was made not behind one of the superpower Niagaras or Hudsons but behind a lowly Mikado.

If we look at the N&W's motive power roster in, say, 1955, we see it neatly divided into two groups. There were the Ys, A-class 2-6-6-4s, and Js (plus the K-2 class 4-8-2s which don't quite fit into any category but most nearly matched the capabilities of the J-class 4-8-4s) — all huge, relatively new, extremely powerful, and as efficient as the technology of the day would permit. Then there were the E-class 4-6-2s, Zs, and M-class 4-8-0s — all old, lightweight, marvelously inefficient, and past the point of being economical to maintain.

The powerful engines were great for taking 11,000 tons into Columbus, racing 15-car passenger trains at 90 miles per hour through the Dismal Swamp, and other heroic feats but not great, in the sense of being efficient, for other tasks. The 5,500 horsepower at 25 miles per hour capability of a newer 2-8-8-2 was as wasted on an eight-car mainline local as much as on a similar train on the Shenandoah Division. Conversely, the older engines whose time was running out, were not efficient for any tasks, save some branch line work where weight restrictions kept the larger engines away and trains were light so as not to overtax a 4-8-0 or 2-6-6-2.

What was needed were locomotives that could be tailored to pull any size load with maximum efficiency. And these tailor-made locomotives could only be constructed by hooking the necessary number of diesel units together as dictated by the train size.

Although the N&W had heretofore followed a "pay-as-you-go" rolling stock and motive power policy, Saunders did not hesitate to borrow $80 million under equipment trust obligations to get his dieselization program into high gear. His reasoning: the money saved would earn the road far more than the 4% or so interest on the trusts. Using the equipment trusts, the N&W took delivery of another 78 diesel units in 1958.

Then, just to get things moving a tad faster, he bumped the K's and J's off all passenger trains by leasing a clutch of RF&P and Atlantic Coast Line E-7 and E-8 diesels in July 1958 for use on Norfolk-Cincinnati varnish. (The Js did get a reprieve late in 1958 when the RF&P and ACL took back their diesels to cover heavier wintertime traffic to Florida). At the same time, Southern Railway diesels began powering the joint N&W-Southern trains between Monroe and Bristol as they had done during the 1950 coal strike. Ironically the Coast Line cab units were older by 5 to 8 years that the newest J's they replaced.

The "pokeberry juice" purple paint scheme of the Coast Line diesels caused hoots of derision from engine crews and train watchers. It also caused consternation in the Roanoke Paint Shop when orders were issued to rustle up some "poke juice" quickly and paint over "Atlantic Coast Line," so that "Norfolk & Western" stencils could be applied. No doubt, these flashy diesels resulted in some headshaking in a Motive Power Department that had previously considered a chaste red stripe bordered in gold on a black engine as the ultimate in daring.

To this furor, Saunders remained indifferent, simply ordering 16 soon-to-be-delivered and six of his existing GP-9s equipped with passenger service steam generators to release the borrowed units. The last of the passenger diesels was received from LaGrange in December 1958.

While they may have lacked the aesthetic appeal of the J-class 4-8-4, the geeps did display a modicum of pizazz. Painted tuscan red to match the road's passenger cars, they sported logos and running board stripes cut from gold reflective paint. Regrettably, they were geared for a maximum speed of 77 miles per hour—a turtle-like gait compared with the 100-plus miles an hour that a J could turn out. But one geep had just the right amount of power for branchline passenger trains and two or sometimes three of them perfectly matched the requirements of mainline varnish.

Despite Saunders' wholehearted endorsement, not everyone in the N&W hierarchy was completely enchanted with diesels. Vice-President H. C. Wyatt, speaking in 1958 before the Mechanical Division of the Association of American Railroads noted that he owned a 20-year old refrigerator that worked perfectly and never required oiling or servicing. Then he added, "I know of few if any individual components on the diesel-electric locomotive that will operate for 20 years without attention." (Why a railroad Vice President would be content with owning a 20-year old refrigerator is a subject beyond the scope of this book.)

Such carping, however, slowed not the tide of dieselization.

By the Spring of 1959, mainline steam—thanks partially to the borrowed Pennsy geeps—had retreated to the east end of the Norfolk Division where a few dirty and ill-maintained 4-6-6-4s continued to lope along the almost gradeless track between Crewe and Norfolk at 50 per with hot shot freights. A few of the Js were also based in Crewe where they were used primarily on local freights. A slightly larger number of Ys were making their last stand in the remote hollows of West Virginia on mine runs out of Iaeger and Williamson. But over the rest of the road the diesel reigned undisputed and supreme. The Roanoke rip track that Summer was clogged with steamers in various stages of dismantlement.

Almost overlooked amidst all this hoopla over road engines was the fact that the N&W did indeed purchase forty 1,000 horsepower Alco T-6 yard switchers to replace almost new 0-8-0s. Despite being geared for a maximum speed of 60 miles per hour, the T-6s seldom ventured outside the yards at Lamberts Point, Roanoke, Bluefield, and Portsmouth so they were frequently overlooked by train watchers. Stuart Saunders' dieselization schedule had to be revised slightly because of an unexpected and fortuitous upturn in business in late 1959. Thus the haunting banshee wail of a 2-8-8-2's whistle regularly continued to bounce off the hillsides in the coal fields around Williamson well into the Spring of 1960.

Then the N&W took delivery of twenty-four 1,800-horsepower EMD GP-18s in the Winter of 1960, putting a total of 529 diesel units on the roster when No. 938, the final GP-18, reached Roanoke on February 6th and General Motors Vice President Richard L. Terrell presented Saunders with a gold-plated locomotive handle. With delivery of these units, no more steamers would be required to meet peak demands. By way of comparison three GP-18s in tandem could just about equal the tractive effort of one Y6b-class 2-8-8-2 at 25 miles per hour.

At 7:20 a.m. May 6, 1960, the last steam-powered freight was dispatched out of Williamson behind Y-6b No. 2190. At 4:00 p.m. that same day, the very last steam locomotive, 0-8-0 No. 291, was dispatched to switch Williamson Yard. That night, the final fires were dropped. Except during a brief visit of ex-Nickel Plate 2-8-4 No. 759 to the Shenandoah and Norfolk Divisions in 1971 and some ferry runs of resuscitated 2-6-6-4 No. 1218 in 1987 and 1988, every pound of freight and every regularly scheduled passenger train has moved over N&W tracks behind diesels since May 6, 1960.

With the possible exception of replacement engines, the story of N&W's dieselization might have ended at this point but Stuart Saunders was not yet through with diesel acquisitions. First, the promise to hold 60 steamers "in reserve," very quickly was dismissed, probably because scrap metal in the early 1960's was bringing a handsome price. Then, there was the realistic expectation that business would continue to increase which dictated the purchase of more motive power.

Although the N&W had banished steam completely with nothing more powerful than an 1,800 horsepower geep, subsequent diesel acquisitions were mostly of much bigger machines — Alco RS-36s in 1962; EMD 2250 horsepower GP-30s in 1962, and 2500 horsepower EMD GP-35s in 1963 and 64, and Alco C-420s in 1964.

When deliveries were slow and motive power shortages threatened, management again took to leasing engines — fifteen 1,500 horsepower F7A and F7B units from the Bessemer & Lake Erie in 1961 and 1962, plus six 2,400 horsepower RS-12s and five SD-9s from the Duluth, Missabe, & Iron range in 1963 and 1964.

It may be argued that these huge new engines, at least in part, negated the advantage of being able to use a number of small diesels to match the tonnage requirements of a particular train. After all, one SD-45 came close to packing the tractive effort of a K-2 class 4-8-2. However, times were changing; the larger diesels simply reflected the needs of increased power and speed for the

Road's expanding coal and merchandise traffic. And the locals of the mid-1950s with but four or five cars were almost a thing of the past ten years later; the humblest way freight now and then need the muscle of a GP-35 to get over the road.

The N&W's operating ratio sank to 57.74% in 1961, the first year of complete dieselization, and by 1966, the road—helped by traffic absorbed from the roads acquired in 1964—posted a net profit of $97,823,000, an amount exceeded only by Union Pacific. A record like that would have been impossible without that "Misbegotten mass of machinery," as the late Lucius Beebe referred to the diesel locomotive. Sentimental stockholders might have settled for a mite less dividends in exchange for the sight and sound and thrill of a 2-8-8-2 thundering on Blue Ridge Grade once more.

Oh by the way, Vice President Wyatt may have been unduly pessimistic when he criticized diesels back there in 1958; some of the GP-9s were still on the N&W's roster three decades later.

N&W Photo, W. E. Warden Coll.

N&W's Dynamometer car is testing brand new GP-9s 11, 12, 14, and 10 probably in late 1955 on the Blue Ridge Grade. Later (in 1956) these units became 710-713.

N&W Photo, W. E. Warden Coll.

Y-6b-class 2-8-8-2 No. 2197 was one of the two steam behemoths that took on the best of LaGrange in the 1952 diesel tests. The Y-6b had a rated tractive effort of 126,838 pounds when operating compound, 152,206 when operating simple.

Norfolk & Western Diesels - 1955-1964
(Based on N&W Motive Power Department Roster dated October 9, 1964)

Road No.	Builder	Class	Horsepower	Date Built
10-39	Alco	T-6	1000	Feb.-Jul. 1959
40-41	Alco	T-6	1000	*(Note 1)*
42-49	Alco	T-6	1000	Sep.-Oct. 1959
200-214	EMD	GP-35	2500	Dec. 1963
215-239	EMD	GP-35	2500	Mar.-Apr. 1964
300-304	Alco	RS-3	1600	Sep.-Oct. 1955 *(Note 2)*
305-307	Alco	RS-3	1600	Jan.-Feb.1956 *(Note 2)*
308-324	Alco	RS-11	1800	Mar.-May 1956
325-340	Alco	RS-11	1800	Jan.-Feb. 1957
341-344	Alco	RS-11	1800	Jun. 1957
345-364	Alco	RS-11	1800	Nov.-Dec. 1957
365-376	Alco	RS-11	1800	Nov.-Dec. 1958
377-400	Alco	RS-11	1800	Jan.-Jun. 1959
401-406	Alco	RS-11	1800	Jun. 1961
407-412	Alco	RS-36	1800	Mar. 1962
500-505	EMD	GP-9	1750	Feb. 1957 *(Note 3)*
506-521	EMD	GP-9	1750	Nov.-Dec. 1958
522-565	EMD	GP-30	2250	Jul.-Sep. 1962
620-639	EMD	GP-9	1750	Nov.-Dec. 1958
640-699	EMD	GP-9	1750	Jan.-Apr. 1959
710-713	EMD	GP-9	1750	Oct. 1955 *(Note 4)*
714-734	EMD	GP-9	1750	Jul. 1956
735-746	EMD	GP-9	1750	Dec. 1956
747-761	EMD	GP-9	1750	Feb. 1957
766, 767	EMD	GP-9	1750	*(Note 5)*
768-812	EMD	GP-9	1750	May 1957
813-842	EMD	GP-9	1750	Mar.-Jun. 1958
843-914	EMD	GP-9	1750	May-Oct. 1959
915-922	EMD	GP-18	1800	Dec. 1959
923-938	EMD	GP-18	1800	Jan. 1960
939-962	EMD	GP-18	1800	Jun.-Sep. 1961

Note 1 - Engines 40 and 41 were sold in July 1963 and October 1964 to subsidiary Chesapeake Western and renumbered CW 10 and 11. Builder's date is August 1959. No. 10 is now property of Virginia Museum of Transportation; No. 11 is the property of the Ronaoke Chapter, National Railway Historical Society.

Note 2 - As built, these units were numbered 92-99, respectively. They were renumbered in the Spring of 1956 as follows:

Old No.	New No.	Old No.	New No.
92	307	96	303
93	306	97	302
94	305	98	301
95	304	99	300

Note 3 - These units as built were intended for freight service; they were subsequently modified with steam generators to allow them to be used on passenger trains.

Note 4 - As built, these units were numbered 10-13. They were renumbered to 710-713 in 1956.

Note 5 - These units were originally Winston-Salem Southbound units No. 1501 and 1502, respectively. Actual builder dates unknown. The WSSB is a partially owned subsidiary of the N&W.

CHESAPEAKE WESTERN - THE N&W'S BACK DOOR TO DIESELDOM

by
William E. Warden
with
C. Grattan Price, Jr.

Don Thomas was an old man and he'd owned the Chesapeake Western Railway for a long time—sixteen years to be exact—and was General Manager for twelve years before that.

Mr. Don was old and ailing and had no heirs to whom he could leave his bucolic 56-mile short line, that wound through Virginia's Shenandoah Valley. He had an almost paternalistic affection for his employees, paying their hospital bills out of his own pocket and helping them out when times were hard. Why, he'd paid for the college education of almost twenty kids in his area. Now he was worried about what would happen to these folks when he became too ill to run the railroad.

Like many another short line, the Chesapeake Western had been projected BIG! Its original builders had proposed to extend it from Tidewater Virginia deep into the West Virginia coal fields, via Elkton and Harrisonburg, Virginia.

The road's westward extension would have involved a series of grades and curves across the Alleghanies that would have given pause to a mountain goat. Crossing the Blue Ridge Mountains east of Elkton at Swift Run Gap to reach Tidewater would have been no piece of cake either. Thus, the CW had to be satisfied to make a living among cornfields, pastures, orchards and woodland of the central Shenandoah Valley.

Size isn't everything and the little road had gained a measure of fame twice in its life span. Back in the early 1930's it had originated free pickup and delivery of less-than-carload freight—a practice subsequently copied by the Pennsylvania Railroad and other rail giants. Then in 1942, it reversed the usual order of things by grabbing up a hunk of Class I railroad—namely, the B&O's moribund Valley Railroad* between Harrisonburg and Staunton, thereby doubling its length overnight.

The Chesapeake Western rails met the Norfolk & Western at Elkton, Virginia, and from that connection received many cars of coal and poultry feed bound for the CW's headquarters city of Harrisonburg, which billed itself as the "Turkey Capital of the World." So when the N&W informed Thomas that they'd like to buy up his line for $825,000 and haul all that poultry feed directly, Mr. Don was right pleased. Now there'd be someone to look after his people.

But first he'd be fair about it. The CW also connected with the Chesapeake & Ohio at Staunton, Virginia, and from that connection received coal and other commodities bound for Harrisonburg and several on-line communities. Hence he told C&O Chesapeake Division General Manager Robert Vawter about the N&W's offer and asked Vawter if the C&O would care to top it.

Heck no, or words to that effect, Vawter replied. The CW was just not the C&O's kind of railroad and the cost of bringing it up to C&O standards of track maintenance, etc., would have been prohibitive.

Well, he'd given them their chance. And on July 29, 1954, the Harrisonburg *News-Record* announced that D. W. Thomas planned to sell his shortline to the N&W subject to ICC approval. ICC approval was easy to come by in those days; the regulatory body okayed the acquisition less than three months later, and on November 10, 1954, in return for payment of $825,000, much in N&W preferred stock, the Chesapeake Western and its three (shh) diesel engines, became a wholly owned subsidiary of the Norfolk & Western—the N&W's first major acquisition of the Merger Age. But with three diesels technically its property how could the N&W continue claiming to be 100 percent steam? Easy. The engines as well as various bridges and other structures continued to be labeled "Chesapeake Western." The track has always borne that kinky look, indicative of having been laid with second—or maybe even third-hand rail. And if you see the Chesapeake Western today and didn't know the whole story, you'd swear you were looking at just another make-do short line (although at this writing most of the line has recently been reballasted.) The C&O may have worried about upgrading the roadbed but such niceties never stopped the N&W from hauling poultry feed to Harrisonburg over track that it would not have tolerated any place else.

The Valley Railroad had its own corporate identity dating back to 1870 when Confederate General Robert E. Lee was its president (in fact this was the only commercial venture in which the General ever took part), but it was leased to the B&O between Harrisonburg and Lexington. Don Thomas had only agreed to purchase it after the B&O received permission to abandon the Staunton-Lexington segment.

VIRGINIAN RAILWAY MERGER A FACTOR IN DIESELIZATION?

Recently, my fellow rail author Robert A. LeMassena made the interesting suggestion that President Stuart Saunders' forced-draft dieselization program had a motive we haven't examined previously—the proposed merger with the Virginian Railway.

A study of the proposed merger began in 1958; Saunders and Virginian President F. D. Beale went public in November of that year with an announcement of the study, stating that "Substantial operating economies could be effected by routing traffic interchangeably over the N&W and Virginian lines to take advantage of the modern yards and terminal facilities and more favorable grades of each railroad. Motive power and cars could be used more efficiently and duplicate facilities eliminated." The announcement added, "This better service, coupled with resultant greater efficiency of operation will be definitely in the public interest." Viewing the merger in retrospect, it would be difficult to quibble over these statements.

LeMassena suggests that savings resulting from dieselization would have driven up the price of N&W stock, thereby allowing the larger road to purchase its neighbor at a lower cost per share of Virginian stock.

Perhaps.

No doubt that dieselization did lower operating cost thereby making the N&W a more attractive long-term investment instrument. What direct effect the diesels had on per-share value would be difficult to say. However, a glance at Table I below, which shows the high and low prices of the stock for the years 1955 through 1959, may give us some clues.

With the exception of 1957, the stock prices were generally trending upward from 1955 through 1958. Since dieselization was under way by the end of 1957, (although not to the extent it would be the following year) the somewhat depressed values of the stock that year would seem to cast doubt on the validity of LeMassena's theory. In 1958, there was a substantial jump in the high price for the year but not in the low price, suggesting that the price rose considerably after the merger and was formally announced. Further, 1959's substantial jump in both the high and low prices suggests that merger announcement was again the driving force behind stock's rise.

Speculation aside, the final terms of the merger were announced early in 1959 - 0.55 shares of Norfolk & Western stock for each share of Virginian common, plus a share-for-share exchange of a new class of N&W preferred for each share of Virginian preferred.

On April 30, 1959 Virginian stockholders voted 99.5% of their shares in favor of the merger. And two weeks later N&W stockholders voted almost 99.7% of their shares the same way. ICC approval was received later that year.

For the Virginian owners, the chief advantage of the merger was that their income would no longer be at the mercy of the vagaries of their lone customer, the coal industry, since the more affluent N&W had a fairly stable and expanding merchandise hauling base. An ancillary advantage was that the catenary, with all its maintenance costs, on the Virginian's electrified main west of Roanoke, could be abandoned. (The final juice-powered train on this main did run June 30, 1962.) But for N&W the advantages were even greater. Not only would the need to boost tonnage over daunting Blue Ridge Grade be eliminated in favor of the Virginian's almost gradeless line from Roanoke to Tidewater, but one of the N&W's major competitors for Pocahontas Coal Region traffic would be eliminated forever. Then too, the N&W would be a more formidable competitor for the remaining Pocahontas road, the Chesapeake & Ohio. These advantages alone would have driven up the stock price regardless of what type motive power the N&W stabled.

It is questionable whether, with these plums dangled before them, the holders would have voted down the merger if there were not a geep on the property and the terms had been as unfavorable as, say, an unlikely share-per-share trade of the common.

In fact they would have been fools if they had.

TABLE I

HIGH AND LOW PRICES OF NORFOLK & WESTERN COMMON STOCK 1955-1959

YEAR	HIGH	LOW
1955	61-7/8	48-1/4
1956	73-3/4	60-1/8
1957	70-3/4	51-1/2
1958	92	53-3/4
1959	108	84-1/4

JAWN HENRY: STEAM'S LAST HURRAH

On May 19, 1954, amid cautious optimism and much fanfare, the Norfolk & Western Railway took delivery of a coal burning steam-powered locomotive numbered 2300, that it hoped would be the first of many that would finally challenge the efficiency and economy of the diesel.

This 586-ton, 161-foot long behemoth of a steam-turbine electric locomotive was quickly dubbed *Jawn Henry*, after the legendary "Steel drivin' man" who did battle with modern technology in the form of a steam drill on the Chesapeake & Ohio's Big Bend Tunnel. Very quickly, *Jawn* proved that he was more than the equal of the N&W's powerful A-class 2-6-6-4s and Y-class 2-8-8-2s in terms of fuel economy both on such hills as Blue Ridge Grade and on the relatively flat line between Williamson and Columbus and Cincinnati. Here at last was a steam locomotive whose fuel costs per ton mile was almost competitive with the best of LaGrange and Schenectady.

But just as the legendary John Henry beat the steam drill, only to "die with the hammer in his hand," this mechanical *Jawn* died an inglorious death after less than four years of service, and was permanently retired on New Years Day 1958.

Two questions: Why a steam-turbine electric? What went wrong? To answer the first question we need a brief course (no pop quizzes) in thermodynamics.

The efficiency of any steam engine, be it in a power plant or in a locomotive, is influenced by, among other things, steam pressure and degrees of superheat. Raise the pressure and the superheating and you increase the efficiency and hence reduce the cost of operating your engine.

Now a reciprocating steam engine is inherently an inefficient machine. The best reciprocating steam locomotives ever built could only boast an efficiency of 7 percent. Sure, in theory, if you could get the steam hot enough and under high enough pressure, that efficiency could be raised somewhat, but practical considerations pretty much limit boiler pressure to about 300 pounds per square inch. Very few steamers, except on an experimental basis, have ever been built with higher pressures. These practical considerations include the fact that the locomotive is subjected continuously to severe shocks and vibrations by the track and its own reciprocating parts. Get the pressure too high and you start springing leaks and causing structural damage.

On the other hand, a steam turbine-driven generator sitting in a power plant typically reaches as high as 30 percent efficiency. It would seem logical that if you add the generator power and electric motor, the efficiency of the turbine-generator-motor combination might be in the order of 20-25-percent. This is true enough but a stationary motor whirling around in a power plant is of small use to anyone. And this efficiency is obtainable only because a turbine in a power plant uses steam at pressures up to 800-1000 p. s. i. and more. You can get away with that in a power plant because the turbine and its boiler are firmly bolted to the floor and vibration and shocks are negligible. But send your power plant rocketing down the tracks at 60 miles per hour and you'd better lower that pressure. Still, even at reduced pressure, the turbine-electric engine ought to be more efficient than a reciprocating one.

There is one problem with a steam turbine, however.

A reciprocating engine is generally content to operate at just about any speed. By properly adjusting throttle and cutoff, it will provide maximum tractive effort at low speeds when the T. E. is needed to accelerate whatever the engine is powering, and at some cruising speed it will deliver less tractive effort but maximum horsepower.

But a turbine is essentially a constant speed device. If you try running it at any but its designed speed, tractive effort (torque in a power plant) will drop off rapidly. This is of no consequence in a power plant as there a turbine runs day and night at one constant speed for which it was designed. However, accelerating a heavy train from a standstill is a slow and inefficient process. The Pennsy tried driving an experimental locomotive directly from a turbine. It was splendidly efficient once the train got up to, say, 60 miles per hour., but when it came to starting up a heavy train, it was no better than one of the road's high-stepping Atlantics.

So, if you are going to use a turbine in a locomotive you must let it run at a more-or-less constant speed and let it drive a generator which in turn powers one or more traction motors that will perform satisfactorily over a range of speeds.

Answering the second question is more difficult.

After observing that other Pocahontas road's experience with a trio of turbine-electrics, purchased to power a flashy daylight Washington-Cincinnati train known as *The Chessie*, why would the N&W even try to create a similar locomotive? Part of the answer was that the C&O turbine-electrics were the brainchild of the Chesapeake & Ohio's flamboyant Chairman and public relations whiz, Robert R. Young. Young ordered three turbine-electrics even though they were an experimental design, and when *The Chessie* was cancelled because of declining passenger business the three monstrous locomotives were used for only a year before being sent to scrap. They had a standard fire-tube boiler, though, and effectively were just a standard steam locomotive boiler turning a turbine to power a generator, with pressure at 310 p. s. i. There were few facilities that could accommodate them and they were to be maintained by people who knew nothing but reciprocating steam, a formula for the disaster that overtook them.

By contrast, N&W management was a lot of things

but nobody ever accused it of being flamboyant. Hard-headed accountants and engineers were making the N&W's motive power decision.

The design and construction of N&W No. 2300 was a combined effort of the N&W and three of the country's leading industrial giants: Baldwin-Lima-Hamilton erected the locomotive, Westinghouse Electric provided the generators and traction motors, and the boiler and turbine were from the respected Babcock and Wilcox.

From the combined effort came a locomotive capable of churning out a maximum of 4,500 drawbar horsepower and reaching a maximum speed of 60 mph. It should be noted that *Jawn* was only more powerful than that road's Y and A class articulated at speeds under about 15 mph. So while his fuel costs were less than either of these two classes, he did take somewhat longer to get from point to point than did trains of comparable weight powered by the Ys and As. But at speeds below 10 mph *Jawn* packed an awesome 144,000 pounds of continuous tractive effort—enough to telescope a steel underframe caboose, which did happen once.

This engine incorporated a variety of features that had never rolled on rails before—nor since. A water tube boiler that eliminated water leaks and staybolts generated 600 p. s. i. steam which hit the turbine blades at 900 degrees Fahrenheit. Each axle of the locomotive's four six-wheel trucks was powered by its own traction motor. Coal was burned on a traveling grate with continuous ash removal. Pressurized combustion air was supplied through an air preheater, thereby eliminating the exhaust nozzle and back pressure on the turbine.

Twenty tons of coal were carried in the locomotive just forward of the boiler. The tender carried only water—22,000 gallons of it—plus a Zeolite water softener. In an emergency, the water softener could be bypassed and water delivered from the tender directly into the boiler. The turbine itself powered two tandem-mounted generators. An to top it off, *Jawn* was equipped with dynamic braking—just like a proper diesel.

Jawn's performance was outstanding, causing president R. H. Smith to tell a gathering of New York security analysts in November 1954 that he saw a "growing future" for the coal industry.

The brass of other railroads followed the tests with considerable interest but to a man declined to follow the N&W into its noble experiment. *Jawn Henry's* initial cost of $800,000 was one deterrent to buying into an unproven form of motive power, even though other rail lines were informed that the cost would come down to $600,000 when *Jawn* clones were produced in quantity. Another deterrent was the fact that the engine efficiency, although better than that of any conventional steam locomotive, never came close to meeting expectation.

Then it was found that some of the complex appliances—particularly one designed to maintain constant boiler pressure regardless of load demands—failed frequently and required constant maintenance and repair. It was this poor maintenance record that finally confined the locomotive to helper service on Blue Ridge Grade, where it could be returned quickly to Roanoke for repairs.

The turbine-electric faced one other problem on account of its enormous length—greater than any other single unit on rails. There were only a few N&W turntables—Roanoke and Bluefield for example—that could accommodate the locomotive. This too limited just where on the N&W *Jawn Henry* could be operated.

Finally, Westinghouse exited the traction motor business and Baldwin-Lima-Hamilton, always a distant fourth in the locomotive business finally went belly up.

It was all these problems—high maintenance costs and down time because of complex machinery, lack of sources for parts, lower than expected efficiency, excessive length, and high initial cost that finally sealed the hapless locomotive's fate. It is interesting to note that when *Jawn* was retired, most of the N&W's super power conventional locomotives were still in service.

Could the steam-turbine electric have ever become the motive power of choice? Possibly, if it had been developed twenty years earlier before the diesel had taken over most of the motive power business and there was more time to debug the complex machinery. For the normally far-sighted N&W however, it was a case of too little and too late.

N&W Photo, Bill Baumgardner Coll.

Jawn Henry powers an eastbound coal drag near Blue Ridge, Virginia, on June 6, 1954, soon after its arrival. Note the dynamometer car partially hidden by the tree.

GENERAL MOTORS VERSUS THE N&W: THE 1952 DIESEL TESTS

The newest, glitziest, freight engine out of LaGrange in 1952 was the F-7. And the last holdout against LaGrange—and Erie and Schenectady (and Eddystone too)—was the Norfolk & Western. What a feather it would be in General Motors' corporate cap if it could crack this last bastion of steam!

In what was certainly a show of good sportsmanship, the N&W agreed to allow GM to demonstrate the prowess of one of its new engines when pitted against the N&W's super power steam. (It has been suggested that the N&W actually "challenged" GM to participate in these tests!)

GM chose an engine that had just completed testing on the Chicago & Northwestern, F-7 No. 459, an A-B-B-A configuration weighing 982,260 pounds on drivers and boasting a starting tractive effort at 25 per cent adhesion of 245,565 pounds and 46,000 pounds (approximately) at 40 mph. By comparison, a Y-6b class 2-8-8-2—the best drag freight hauler that the Roanoke Shops had to offer —had a starting tractive effort of 152,206 pounds operating simple and approximately 42,000 pounds at 40 mph. Comparable figures for the A-class 2-6-6-4 were 114,000 and approximately 50,000 pounds. The diesel demonstrator was geared for a maximum speed of 65 mph (gear ratio of 62:15.) Maximum speeds for the Y6b and the A were approximately 50 and 75 mph, respectively.

Each of the demonstrator's units was equipped with a two-cycle engine capable of delivering 1,500 crankshaft horsepower, and with four traction motors, each pair of motors being supported by a fully flexible truck and each truck containing four 40" diameter wheels.

The overall length of the four diesel units over coupler faces was 201 feet 4 inches and the fuel tanks topped off at 4,800 gallons. In addition, the demonstrator carried 800 gallons of lubricating oil, 64 cubic feet of sand, and 890 gallons of cooling water.

Getting test details from the N&W is not easy. General Manager of Motive Power and Equipment, Clarence Pond, when asked for information about the 1952 tests, politely but firmly told one inquiring author back in 1965, "We have never made it a practice to give widespread distribution of tests conducted on our Railway on various types of equipment and the same policy will be followed in this case." Hence, much of what follows is based on the

General Motors' official test report issued in November 1952.

Tests were run between September 9 – 27 on the Scioto (Williamson to Portsmouth non-stop) and Pocahontas (Williamson to Bluefield with a stop at Farm) Divisions. Additionally, tests were run between Farm and Bluefield, where the ruling grade on Elkhorn Grade was 1.4%, with the diesels acting as pushers with a 2-8-8-2 on the point. (Ruling grade between WIlliamson and Farm was 0.6%) GM, perhaps a bit awed by the N&W's steam prowess, thought that there was a niche on the railway for diesel helpers and said so in their report. Remember, back in 1952, diesel power was still the new kid on the block—albeit a powerful bully growing up rapidly—as far as rail freight was concerning, particularly among the Pocahontas roads, and a foot in any door was better than no foot at all.

Perhaps GM had a point there. Using the F-7 as a helper, a Y6b could take an 8,300 ton train into Bluefield from the west, whereas 2-8-8-2s pushing and pulling together were limited to 6,600 tons. A diesel-steam combination would, in GM's words, "Save one 6,600-ton train every four trips." GM further opined that with F-7s fore and aft 10,000 ton trains could be hauled from Williamson to Bluefield with the 98-mile run requiring approximately five hours.

Helper service aside, the F-7 performed well, albeit not sensationally.

During the first five days of the test, the demonstrator hauled 175-car coal trains (about 15,500 tons) from Williamson to Portsmouth in competition with 2-6-6-4 No. 1239. This approximated the rated load (approximately 16,000 tons) for a 2-6-6-4 on this 111-mile stretch of track. On one test run, the demonstrator made the trip in 3 hours and 11 minutes, start to stop, for an average running speed of 34.5 miles an hour. With a 14,500 ton train, a 2-6-6-4 frequently made this trip in as little as 3 hours and 20 minutes. And during three test runs, the 1239 running at rated load (i.e. 16,000 tons) made it in 3 hours and 31 minutes. Perhaps most significantly the fuel cost per MGTM was almost identical for the diesel and the 1239. Table I below compares some typical test results. Both east and westbound trains averaged 175 cars but eastbound consists are made up primarily of

TABLE I

Section	Distance	A Load	A Time	Diesel Demonstrator Load	Diesel Demonstrator Time
Williamson-Portsmouth	111 miles	16,028 tons	3 hrs 31 min	15,763 tons	3 hrs 33 min
Portsmouth-Williamson	111miles	4,130 tons	3 hrs 08 min	4,126 tons	3 hrs 11 min

13

empty hoppers. Times are start-to-stop running time.

Fuel costs were less for the Diesel than for the 1239. Savings ranged from a high of 8% eastbound to 15% westbound. So, yes, the F-7 performed better than an A, but not enough better to justify the capital outlay for diesel locomotivs and fueling and servicing facilities to replace the two-year old steamers. And unofficially, the GM test engineers allowed as how they'd made a few custom "modifications" to finagle approximately 1,700 horsepower out of each unit.

The Pocahontas Division with its sawtooth profile was almost exclusively the province of the hard-slogging 2-8-8-2s and here the demonstrator was pitted against less-than-year-old 2-8-8-2 No. 2197. Aside from the afore mentioned pusher experiment, the tests were again almost a standoff with regard to tonnage ratings of the two locomotives.

Where the F-7 did stand out was in its ability to get across the steeper parts of this grade faster than its competition. This was primarily due to the diesels almost limitless tractive effort at low speeds. The Y6b's starting tractive effort when operating simple (i.e., with high pressure steam fed directly to the low pressure cylinders) was approximately 170,000 pounds, whereas that of the 459 was a whopping 245,565 pounds. It was only at higher speeds—say above 20 mph—that the steamer had a tractive effort edge over the demonstrator.

Paradoxically, on the steep down grade from Bluefield to Farm—where tractive effort counts for naught—the demonstrator could also get a train over the road quicker than could the 2197, thanks to the diesel's dynamic brakes. On this 1.4% downgrade, the 459 could hold trains up to 5,000 tons with no application of airbrakes or car retainers—something no steamer could do. This translated into improved wheel life and also reduced running time, as with dynamic braking there was not the usual wait for air brake release before a train could be brought up to track speed.

Some idea of just what the 459 accomplished on the Pocahontas Division can be gleaned from Table II which compares Y6b and diesel loads and start-to-stop running times.

TABLE II

Section	Distance	Y6b		Diesel Demonstrator	
		Load	Tim	Load	Time
Williamson-Farm	62 miles	7,481 tons	2 hrs 31min.	7,422 tons	2 hrs 29 min
Farm-Bluefield	36 miles	3,818 tons	1 hr. 40 min.	5,184 tons	2 hrs 02 min

NOTE: Y6b tonnage ratings - Williamson-Farm 4,500; Farm-Bluefield 3,600.

With both locomotives hauling trains of approximately 7,500 tons (typical of the tonnage of manifest freight No. 86) the 459 had a fuel saving of approximately 6% between Williamson and Farm. But with comparable tonnage between Farm and Bluefield fuel costs were actually less for the 2197. However the diesel could haul 35% greater tonnage up Elkhorn Grade with 10% less fuel per MGTM.

What did all this testing prove?

Not much on the Scioto Division but on the Pocahontas Division, the demonstrator could put out more gross ton miles per train hour on steep grades than a Y6b and at a lower fuel cost.

In terms of gross ton miles and fuel cost, it would appear that there was a definite place for diesels, at least between Farm and Bluefield.

But in terms that a comptroller could understand, the steamers were all paid for and the idea of getting involved in diesel locomotive equipment trusts and constructing new servicing facilities was anathema to management. Corporately, the N&W told GM thanks but no thanks and the 459 went on to its new owner, the Union Pacific.

A smart move or blind devotion to steam? Many years after the fact, N&W Manager of News and Community Service, the late Ben Dulaney, wrote as follows to the author concerning GM's report: "I don't think the report proves much except that it [the 459] was a pretty good 6,000 horsepower diesel. President Smith of course decided it was not for us — and he was so right."

Everything considered, we tend to agree with Ben.

E. A. Honeycutt Coll.

6,000 Horsepower EMD demonstrator No. 459 rolls into Bluefield back in September 1952. The diesels performed well on the N&W's main between Bluefield and Portsmouth but not well enough to make the N&W give up on allegiance to steam.

Norfolk & Western Steam Locomotives
April 1, 1954

Road No.	Builder(Date)	Type	Class	Drivers (inches)	Tractive Effort
6-7	BLW(1897)	2-8-0	G1	50	29,376
100-115	Roanoke(1916-17)	4-8-2	K1	70	62,920
116-125	Alco(Brooks)(1919)	4-8-2	K2	70	63,932
126-137	BLW(1923)	4-8-2	K2a	70	63,932
200-244	Roanoke(1951-53)	0-8-0	S1a	52	62,932
255-284	BLW(1948)(ex-C&O)	0-8-0	S1	52	62,932
375,376,379,382,396 405,422,429,433,444, 449,451,475,477,488, 496	Alco(Rich.)& BLW(1906-07)	4-8-0	M	56	40,163
544,563,578	Alco(Rich.) (1910-14)	4-6-2	E2a	70	34,425
600-613	Roanoke(1941-50)	4-8-4	J	70	80,000
800,809,821	BLW(1898-1900)	0-8-0T	W6	56	40,163
830	BLW(1900)	0-8-0T	W6	56	40,163
1105,1115,1117,1119, 1120,1124,1125,1127- 1129,1138,1139,1143, 1148	BLW(1910-11)	4-8-0	M2	56	52,457
1150,1152,1154,1155, 1157,1159	Roanoke(1911-12)	4-8-0	M2a	56	52,457
1200-1243	Roanoke(1936-50)	2-6-6-4	A	70	114,000
1331,1339,1342,1351,1355,1363,1367, 1375,1377,1381,1383,1392,1397,1398, 1402,1404,1406,1407,1409,1417,1418, 1420,1428,1429,1438,1440,1442-1448, 1451,1452,1454-1456,1458-1463,1465, 1470,1471,1474-1476,1478-1484,1487- 1489	Alco(Rich.)(Schen.), &BLW (1912-1918)	2-6-6-2	Z1a/b	57	90,996
2001-07,2009-12,2016-19, 2023-24,2028,2031-33, 2037-40,2043-45,2047-49	Alco & BLW (1919)	2-8-8-2	Y3	58	136,985
2050-2079	Alco(Rich.)(1923)	2-8-8-2	Y3a	58	136,985
2080-2089	Alco(Rich.)(1927)	2-8-8-2	Y4	58	136,985
2101-2119	Roanoke(1930-32)	2-8-8-2	Y5	58	152,206
2120-2154	Roanoke(1936-40)	2-8-8-2	Y6	58	152,206
2155-2170	Roanoke(1942)	2-8-8-2	Y6a	58	152,206
2171-2200	Roanoke(1948-52)	2-8-8-2	Y6b	58	152,206

Norfolk to Roanoke

William E. Warden

One of the N&W's ubiquitous S-1 class 0-8-0 switchers, No. 262, is shunting cars on an industrial siding in downtown Norfolk, early on a June 1955 morning. The N&W purchased the 262 and 29 of her sisters from the rapidly dieselizing C&O and liked the design so much that an additional 45 almost identical 0-8-0s, labeled S-1a class, were built in the Roanoke Shops between 1951 and 1953. Of significance is the fact that the last steam locomotive in regular service on the N&W was an S-1a.

If you never saw a yard switcher like Alco T-6 class No. 13, do not feel bad. Alco built only 57 of these yard goats between 1958 and 1969 and 40 of them went to the N&W to replace 0-8-0 steam switchers, some of which were built as late as 1953. The N&W's T-6s spent most of their time in various important yards including Lamberts Point (shown here), Bluefield, and Roanoke. Behind No. 13 are two passenger Geeps, Nos. 517 and 517 (see next page).

William E. Warden

William E. Warden

Before the Alco T-6 diesels took over shifter duties in such yards as Lamberts Point (Norfolk), Roanoke, and Bluefield, the N&W did most of its switching with jaunty S-1 and S-1a class 0-8-0s, of which 258, busy about chores at Lamberts Point in June 1955, was typical of the former class. As mentioned above, N&W bought the S-1s from the C&O, paying a bargain $45,000 each, making them the last steam locomotives the road bought from a commercial builder (Baldwin had built them for the C&O).

16

Passenger GP-9s Nos. 518 and 517 (wearing the latter-day "half-moon" paint scheme), have just been pulled into Lamberts Point servicing facility by Alco T-6 switcher No. 13, just visible at the extreme right in May 1970.

William E. Warden

Class A 2-6-6-4 No. 1220 is seen here hurrying fast freight Train No. 78 along a well maintained N&W mainline east of Nottoway, Virginia on March 22, 1956.

N&W Photo, K. L. Miller Coll.

Even a non-railfan would have to admit that although GP-9s Nos. 759 and 686 are probably more efficient than the Class A shown above, they're not nearly so interesting or dramatic as they whip around a curve also near Nottoway with a 150-car coal train. Destination: Norfolk; where else?

Curt Tillotson, Jr.

At left, GP-9 No. 690, RS-11 No. 330, and GP-9 No. 878 are waiting at the west end of Crewe Yard with 220 empty hopper cars for permission to leave for Roanoke, while at right a pair of Geeps putters about the yard. December 1962.

One of N&W's rare (i. e., only five on the roster) RS-36s, No. 409, trails GP-9 No. 730 on a 93-car local eastbound freight just west of Blackstone. The RS-36s were added to the roster in March 1962, long after the last steamer had been retired, and thus didn't figure in the N&W's dieselization. Taken in October 1963.

In December 1962, the westbound *Pocahontas* behind GP-9s Nos. 500 and 516 pauses at Crewe, Virginia. The switcher in the background has just added a diner to the abbreviated consist. Are two Geeps really necessary on this train? For mastering the east slope of Blue Ridge Grade and hewing to the schedule, the answer is yes.

(**Above**) Crewe Yard was still a busy place in November 1962 as GP-9 No. 770 and RS-11 No. 311 wait with a trainload of coal bound for Norfolk's Lamberts Point piers. The black diamonds are headed for Europe and will stay here in the yard until the collier at Norfolk is ready to load them aboard.

(**Below**) The eastbound *Pocahontas* whipping through Burkeville, Virginia in the late 1960s.

(Above) Awaiting another run to Durham, RS-3 No. 97 burbles quietly at Lynchburg, Virginia. In the Spring of 1956, the Alco was renumbered 303.

(Left) In a scene that typified Blue Ridge Grade in the steam days, A-class 2-6-6-4 No. 1228 is going all out to lift yet one more eastbound freight across the grade. Although not intended as a mountain engine, the 2-6-6-4s made a good accounting of themselves on the N&W's sawtooth profile east of Roanoke and at this point, the 1228's tractive effort just about matches that of the helper 2-8-8-2 a mile downgrade. A 2-6-6-4 on the point plus a 2-8-8-2 helper made the ideal combination for getting fast freight out of Roanoke in what the late David P. Morgan characterized as "Steam's Finest Hour." Photo taken in July 1958.

20

2-6-6-4 No. 1224 is doing what it did best—spliting the wind with westbound manifest freight. We are at Bedford, Virginia, and the 1224 came into view just seconds after the photographer had screeched the Plymouth to a halt at this location, jumped out of the car, and aimed his camera at the track in August 1956.

William E. Warden

K-1 class 4-8-2 No. 108 digs in and local westbound freight tied to its tender comes to life on the grade at Bedford, Virginia, in July 1956. In the author's estimation, the K-1s would have been handsome engines were it not for the bulbous air reservoir on the pilot deck.

William E. Warden

With an abbreviated eastbound *Pocahontas* in tow, GP-9s 510 and 502 sprint along the relatively flat trackage near Thaxton, Virginia in May 1959. Between the two main tracks, is a pusher track, a reminder of steam days, when straining 2-8-8-2 pushcrs would be uncoupled near here and then drift down to Boaz to await another assignment.

N&W, VPI&SU Coll.

Train No. 4, *The Pocahontas*, eastbound at Montvale, Virginia has GP-9s 519 and 511 to carry a 12-car train swollen with holiday travelers on December 12, 1958.

N&W, VPI&SU

2-6-6-4 No. 1231 blasts around another curve at Blue Ridge Grade with an eastbound freight in October 1957. Ere another October comes, this volcanic eruption and its accompanying shotgun exhaust will be memories on Blue Ridge—replaced with the snarl of GP-9s and RS-11s.

William E. Warden

(Left) A set of five GP-9s, headed by No. 637 with a manifest freight at Thaxton, Virginia, August 24, 1959. The N&W skillfully retouched this official photo to bring out the logo, number, and engineer.

N&W, VPI&SU

(Below) N&W 4-8-4 No. 611 running out its final few miles in revenue service before retirement, comes bounding up Blue Ridge Grade on a muggy August 1959 Sunday. Behind the locomotive are some 15 cars filled with Appalachian Power Company employees bound for a Virginia Beach vacation. Train is eastbound at some 40 mph. Within five minutes of this photograph, train had accelerated to 70 mph on the relatively level track east of Blue Ridge.

William E. Warden

Southern Railway diesel No. 6130 leads the eastbound *Tennessean,* one of the jointly operated N&W/SR passenger trains, up Blue Ridge Grade after Presidents Stuart T. Saunders had ordered all steam locomotives off passenger trains on *his* railroad. Southern diesels had operated the joint trains between Monroe and Bristol during the 1950 coal miners' strike so this scene was purely a case of deja vu. Photographed August 1958.

23

William E. Warden

A manifest freight sweeps around that long curve at Blue Ridge Grade behind GP-9s (left to right) No. 784, 807 and 675. A mile or so behind are another trio of GP-9s shoving on the caboose. Note the two army tanks–probably bound for Ft. Pickett in eastern Virginia–on the second car behind the diesels. Photographed August 1959.

William E. Warden

It would have taken more than dieselization to eliminate the need for helpers on Blue Ridge Grade back in August 1959. Three geeps headed by 634 and 783 perform the same task that a 2-8-8-2 would have been performing twelve months earlier.

William E. Warden

The Norfolk & Western borrowed 30 Pennsylvania Railroad geeps when it couldn't get fast enough delivery of ordered units. Here are four of the Pennsy growlers, headed by No. 7207, starting up Blue Ridge grade with an eastbound manifest in October 1957.

William E. Warden

Y6a-class 2-8-8-2 No. 2145, lately bumped off the Shenandoah Division by diesel power, here does one of the things she does best – assists an eastbound freight across Blue Ridge Grade. Photographed October 1957.

William E. Warden

In a scene long gone, but not forgotten by those who witnessed it, doubleheaded 2-8-8-2s go stomping by Blue Ridge Grade with another eastbound coal drag. More than a mile downgrade, a third 2-8-8-2 is thrusting all its tractive effort on the drag's cabin car. Y6b-class No. 2175 will cut loose on the fly from the train about half a mile past this spot. The aft helper will disconnect just about where we are. But for the moment 18,000 horsepower worth of Mallets is once again moving coal. Photographed October 1957.

William E. Warden

25

Crew of N&W 4-8-2 No. 112 mug for photographer as the burly K1-class mountain whips around curve at Blue Ridge with bobtailed Lynchburg-Roanoke local. Once, many years ago, the 112 whipped the *Pocahontas* around this same curve. But it is a tribute to the mechanical perfection of this 1917 product of the Roanoke Shops can still earn its keep on the October 1957 afternoon. Note that an ex-C&O tender trails the engine.

At almost exactly the same spot as above, RS-11 helpers No. 356, 320, 314 at Blue Ridge drifting downgrade to the Boaz pusher siding after completing one more helper assignment. Back in those waning days of 1957, one could see an interesting mix of steam and diesels on the Grade. Photographed December 1957.

GP-9s No. 728 and 737 scamper around the same curve at the crest of Blue Ridge Grade with a westbound local. The size of the bobtailed train would seem to indicate that one geep would have provided adequate motive power, particularly as most of the cars were dropped off between Lynchburg and here. Photographed December 1957.

(all) William E. Warden

26

Leased RF&P passenger diesel (E-8) No. 1014 (lettered for N&W) guides the eastbound *Pocahontas* through a curve at Blue Ridge. Symbolic of the transition from Steam to diesel, Y-6 class 2-8-8-2 No. 2142 waits patiently in a siding with a local freight for passage of the proud streamliner. Photographed September 1958.

With a switch stand posing like a loney sentinal, J-class 4-8-4 No. 611 is wheeling a bobtailed *Powhatan Arrow* through the Virginia countryside between Lynchburg and Roanoke in May 1958 just about a month before leased RF&P and ACL E-7s and E-8s took over the varnish until N&W's passenger GP-9s could be delivered. Who could have guessed then that 611 would be carrying passengers in 1991 as an excursion locomotive!

We're somewhere around Bonsack as Y-6 class 2-8-2 No. 2134 shoves on the cabin car of an eastbound freight, while in the background Z-1 class 2-6-6-2 heads up a work train. At this late date, the marvelously inefficient Z-1s were a rare sight on the N&W main, but a few could still be found on work trains and in switching service. Photographed November 1956.

William E. Warden Coll.

One of the more obscure groups of diesels – obscure because they seldom wandered past yard limits–were the Alco T-6 class 1,000 horsepower yard diesels of which No. 30 here in Roanoke passenger station, is an example. Actually the T-6's were geared for 60 mph which is high stepping for a yard goat.

William E. Warden

A trio of GP-9s, Nos. 737, 747 and 778, thread their way through Roanoke yard with a northbound freight on a rainy July 1957 day. Roanoke passenger station is just behind the highway bridge.

William E. Warden

ONE ERA ENDS—ANOTHER BEGINS

(Above) The last steam-powered *Pocahontas* (with J-class 4-8-4 No. 610) and the first diesel-powered one **(below)** rumble across the diamond just east of the Roanoke passenger station on, respectively, the 17th and 18th of July, 1958. Diesels are leased RF&P E-8s still lettered for that road. They will be relettered N&W shortly for the duration of their stay. In the lower photo, it's interesting to note the J-powered eastbound *Powhatan Arrow* being worked as the *Pocahontas* arrives.

(Below) Steam's answer to the diesel challenge? N&W management hoped so. In 1947 they modified two M2-class 4-8-0s (Baldwin, 1910), No. 1100 and 1102, in an attempt to create a steam switcher that could provide the improved thermal efficiency, high availability, and low maintenance of diesels at a fraction of the investment. The two locomotives were given higher-capacity tenders, longer combustion chambers, low speed stokers, and turbine-driven draft fans. Automatic boiler pressure controls reduced the need for human attendance. Although these experimental switchers performed as hoped for, purchase of the C&O's surplus but almost new 0-8-0s prevented further experimentation, and the 1100 and 1102 were retired in 1951. Here 1100 is at Shafers Crossing shortly after being outshopped. The odd casing over domes, stack, and bell was largely cosmetic.

William E. Warden

(Above) New Passenger GP-9s, Nos. 512 and 515, are being checked out at Shaffers Crossing terminal in Februray 1959. The A-class 2-6-6-4 No. 1210, in steam at right was definitely an oddity in Roanoke at this time. Beit guess is that it was sent here from Crewe for some emergency repairs that the Crewe shop couldn't accommodate and that it will be eastbound shortly.

T. W. Dixon Coll.

William E. Warden

Roanoke's "other" passenger station, the Virginian Railway depot at right hadn't seen much traffic in years, but these days most eastbound freight was traveling over the old Virginian low-grade main east of Roanoke, so a great many trains, although not stopping here, did pass the station. This coal drag is distinguished by being partially powered by Alco RS-3 No. 305 (middle unit), one of only eight RS-3s the N&W owned and one of the very first diesels the road purchased, way back in February 1956. On the point is RS-11 No. 366 which first burnished N&W rails in November 1958. The date is June 1967.

30

The Shenandoah Line

A few miles out of Roanoke on the Shenandoah Division is Cloverdale, Virginia, where this meet was captured by the N&W's official photographer on August 7, 1959, with shiny GP-9s on both trains.

N&W, VPI&SU

Five Geeps lead by Nos. 893 and 668, haul a mile of high cars up the long grade south of Waynesboro, Virginia, and into Lyndhurst. The Blue Ridge Mountains almost crowd down to trackside. Photo taken in April 1963.

(both) William E. Warden

Say, isn't that pair of Geeps heading a local on the Shenandoah Disivion. Well, yes, but - Hey, wasn't one of the purposes of dieselizing the Shenandoah Division so that motive power could be matched to consists? Yes but - Then why are 777 and 691 rolling southward through Sampson with only nine cars? Surely one GP-9 would suffice? Well yes, but when they left the Shenandoah Division point they might have had 35-40 cars, but after dropping some covered hoppers at Elkton for the CW, maybe these nine are all that's left! The train may pick up more at Waynesboro as well.

31

In another—and some might say kinder and gentler—time, K2a-class 4-8-2 No. 130, a 1923 product of Baldwin, accelerates Train No. 1, the "New York Train" south of Waynesboro, Virginia, in June 1956. The author still has fond memories of business and pleasure trips aboard a steam-powered No. 1, and its northbound counterpart, No. 2. Now compare this scene with the same train and location three years later (below) as GP-9 No. 500 accelerates the train out of town. What a difference!

Many years have passed since this many people gathered to board an N&W train at Waynesboro, nor have there been this many cars on a Shenandoah Division passenger train in probably 10 years. Diesels 520 and 514 are leading the "GOP Special" loaded with Republicans going to their annual state convention in Roanoke in October 1960. The actual station was torn down two years earlier and all that remains in this scene are the steps and foundation next to the nearest express wagon. Regular patrons of trains Nos. 1 and 2 did their waiting upstairs in the C&O station from whose track this picture was taken.

Crew of GP-9 No. 500 have little to do but watch baggage and mail unloaded from Shenandoah Division Train No. 1 at Waynesboro. The scene will be repeated in half a dozen small towns before the train reaches Roanoke. This heavy head-end business accounted for the 2 hours and 42 minutes it took No. 1 to traverse the 96 miles between Waynesboro and Roanoke, but it allowed No. 1 and its northbound counterpart to provide overnight sleeping car accommodations between Roanoke and New York City via a connection with the Pennsy at Hangerstown, Maryland, plus a better-than-average dining car. When Nos. 1 and 2 finally lost their mail and expreess contracts the Roanoke-Waynesboro running time was cut to a more reasonable 2 hours and 16 minutes. Inexplicably, the Waynesboro-Roanoke time was left at 2 hours and 40 minutes!

(both) William E. Warden

M-2 class 4-8-0 No. 1119 is about her appointed task of switching cars in the Waynesboro yard. The M-2's 56-inch drivers make it hard to believe that this locomotive was originally designed for fast freight service. But in the days when a long freight train was 30 cars and "fast" meant 40 mph, the 4-8-0s (of which the N&W had more than any other railroad) were ideally suited for this service. In later days they were used as switchers.

This impressive machine, M-2 class 4-8-0 No. 1119, was the regular yard goat at Waynesboro in pre-diesel days. How many steam switchers ever boasted four-wheel pilot trucks and 12-wheel tenders almost as long as the engine? Baldwin outshopped her in 1910, yet she outlasted N&W steamers many years her junior.

Riding the turntable at Shenandoah, Virginia, is one of the last K-1 class 4-8-2s in operation. It was then used for local freight between Shenandoah and Hagerstown. A kindly yardmaster had ordered the 114 brought out of the roundhouse and parked on the turntable. The photographer's wife, Claire, was then allowed to operate the turntable controls and positioned the locomotive so that it caught all the early morning Winter sun on this cold January day in 1957.

(all) William E. Warden

34

Snow in Virginia? Why of course, we're not in the corn pone and palmetto belt but rather, in the Shenandoah Valley, whose elevation gives it winter temperatures similar to those of Cape May, New Jersey, but with considerably less humidity. Jumbo flakes of wet, sticky snow are falling as GP-9 No. 842 tries to break loose from the white stuff clogging Waynesboro yard and tries to get through to Shenandoah before things get worse. Propane burners heat the switch points to keep them from getting clogged. And what was an idiot rail photographer doing out on a day like this? Why being an idiot rail photographer, of course. The date is January 1966.

(both) William E. Warden

It is a bright Spring morning and Y-6 class 2-8-8-2 No. 2143 is loping across a field at Waynesboro with a northbound manifest in June 1956. In those days, the photographer could crawl out of the house on a Saturday morning, photograph this train and its soundbound counterpart, at least one local freight, the southbound Hagerstown-Roanoke varnish, and the Waynesboro yard switcher—all in steam—and be back home in time for breakfast. There is no indication here that the last steam locomotive would depart Waynesboro in another eight months.

It's a bright Spring morning in 1956 as Y-6 2-8-8-2 No. 2143 wheels a northbound freight around a curve in Waynesboro. Just out of sight to the right is the General Electric Company's Specialty Control Department plant. The scene below is similar, but after dieselization.

Highball! This northbound freight has just gotten the green signal at Waynesboro and is off for Hagerstown and points north behind four RS-11s. Compare this action with that above. The large two-story building at left is General Electric's Specialty Control Department. When Specialty Control opened in 1955, the N&W anticipated considerable new business and even partied local GE officials. Alas, the Department's products (electromechanical relays, aircraft electrical systems, and machine controls) moved primarily by truck. The building at right with the curved roof is an old airplane hanger inasmuch as the GE plant was built on the site of the former Waynesboro airport!

(both) William E. Warden

On the basis of one picture being worth a thousand words, we present herewith one of the most cogent arguments for dieselization we know of. The time is October 1955 and this three-car northbound local at Waynesboro is marvelously overpowered by Y-6a 2-8-8-2 No. 2165. One GP-9 would have been more than sufficient for the job, but alas, the big Mallet was the only thing in the roundhouse. Diesels can be used as building blocks, additional units added until enough power is attained, but with big steam like the N&W used, it was hard to match smaller jobs.

A mile of southbound freights eases into Waynesboro on a Sunday afternoon behind a conglomeration of motive power, GP-9s 668 and 893, an unidentifiable GP-9, GP-18 No. 952, and another unit that appears to be a T-6 class yard switcher. The N&W and C&O interchanged cars at Waynesboro, but since switching is normally a Monday-thru-Saturday proposition, those C&O hoppers will stay where they are until tomorrow. The date is April 1963.

Geeps No. 825 and 748 and another unit wheel a southbound freight around a curve on Shenandoah Division's track at Port Republic, Virginia. A glance at the consist of this train gives some idea of the variety of merchandise moved over the Shenandoah line in June 1963.

(all) William E. Warden

Block signals frame GP-9 No. 656 as it rolls a northbound local through Port Republic on the N&W's Shenandoah Division. Nearby, the track crosses the site of a Civil War battlefield. Photographed on June 2, 1963.

(both) William E. Warden

Five diesels are muscling a manifest freight across the trestle that bridges Stoney Run, one of the many tributaries that empty into the South Fork of the Shenandoah River. We are not far from the metropolis of Stanley, Virginia, on this beautiful November 1963 afternoon. The encrustation of dirt on the Geeps' flanks makes identification almost impossible, indicating that diesels have indeed become just like their work-a-day steam predecessors, weathered in their work.

West of Roanoke

N&W GP-9 733 in company with three leased PRR Geeps has an empty hopper train in tow at Pepper, Virginia, long a favorite location for official photos. Note the center siding and the full over-the-track signal bridge in the background. Taken May 27, 1958.

(both) N&W, VPI&SU

GP-9 No. 750, long hood forward as was N&W standard practice, along with leased Pennsylvania Railroad Geeps 7201 and 7226, powers an eastbound coal train at Elliston, Virginia, May 28, 1958, framed by a typical N&W signal mast and cantilever signal bridge.

N&W GP-9 No. 722 leads a pair of leased Pennsy Geeps up Christiansburg Hill with a manifest freight in June 1958, when EMD wasn't delivering diesels fast enough for N&W.

H. H. Harwood, Jr.

A cantilever signal bridge looms over manifest freight headed by GP-9 783 at Walton, Virginia. Near here the Bristol line diverges from the main. Photographed December 13, 1957.

Four GP-9s with a freight round a bend in the famous New River region near Narrows, Virginia, during the later dieselization period (No. 638 was delivered in December 1959).

Again along the New River near Narrows in 1958, three leased PRR Geeps led by No. 7206 power a mixed freight train with merchandise cars up front and coal on the rear.

(all) N&W, VPI&SU

40

This often-reproduced publicity photo shows J-class 4-8-4 No. 607 hard by the New River at Parrott, Virginia with the *Powhatan Arrow* about 1950. This was the image of the N&W in its era of superpower steam before it finally gave way to diesels and replaced the beauty and power of the Js with the boxy Geeps.

(both) N&W. VPI&SU

A common sight on the N&W's Radford Division back in August 1956 was an endless train of loaded hoppers passing an equally endless train of empties, for the railway, like its Pocahontas neighbors, was a busy conveyor belt for coal. Y-6b class 2-8-8-2 No. 2179 was doing the honors near Pearisburg, Virginia, with the eastbound coal drag. Backhauling empty hoppers did nothing to enhance the bottom line on a profit-and-loss statement—even on a cash-happy road like the N&W.

An eastbound freight headed by GP-9 No. 781, cruses along New River near Narrows in the Summer of 1960. In an earlier a 2-8-8-2 would have been on the point rather than this quartet of internal combustion machines.

(Above) Another eastbound coal train threads its way through the New River Gorge behind GP-18 No. 924 and GP-9s No. 851 and 914 (the latter the last GP-9 delivered to the N&W), and an unidentified Geep. It is difficult to differentiate between GP-9s and GP-18s. The latter packed an additional 50 horsepower. But the best way to tell one type from the other is by the engine number.

(Right) A westbound N&W freight, led by GP-9 No. 648, ducks under the Virginian Railway bridge across the New River at Glen Lyn, Virginia. A pair of Fairbanks-Morse Trainmasters is on the point of a Virginian hopper train, August 6, 1959. the N&W-VGN marriage would be consumated less than four months later on December 1, 1959. Did the upcoming marriage have anything to do with the rapid dieselization of the N&W? One rail author thinks so.

Alco RS-11 No. 313 is getting a good scrubbing in the diesel washer at Bluefield. Engine No. 355 has just completed the bath. Note the boards covering all the vents. The idea: to keep water out of the engine's innards. The inverted-J ductwork at left is a steam-era leftover. It used to trap the exhust of steam locomotives that would otherwise have dirtied up Bluefield residents' clothes. A city ordinance dictated the use of this device.

N&W, VPI&SU

William E. Warden

GP-9s 674 and 634, plus two other units, led a train of empty hoppers west at Bluefield, Virginia. A couple of Alco units at far left are engaged in yard switching. The huge coaling tower is mostly idle these days as the diesels have a lock on freight as far west at Williamson when this photo was taken in October 1959.

Although she's probably sat in the same spot at Bluefield yard hundreds of times before, Y-6a 2-8-8-2 No. 2174 looks strangely uncomfortable and out-of-place with Alcos and Geeps on adjacent track. But then steam has been absent from Bluefield for almost a year now and the only reason for the 2174 is there on this July 1959 is (as the camera-laden characters on the track attest) a trip of the "Rail Museum Safari" excursion train from Roanoke to Iaeger.

William E. Warden

Snow blankets the Bluefield yard in January 1958 but there is not enough of the white stuff to make any difference so far as freight transportation was concerned. Alco RS-18s power a train at left while GP-9s are on the right.

Joe Schmitz

N&W, VPI&SU

A variety of motive power is present at the Bluefield engine terminal in July 1956. The smoke abatement equipment mentioned in an earlier caption is in full use here in the background at left. The state line ran through the middle of Bluefield, leaving the primary portion of the town and N&W in West Virginia, with a smaller one in Virginia.

Freight traffic on the Winston-Salem line was heavy on this August 1958 day as this freight lead by GP-9 No. 832 and three of her sisters attests.

We are deep in Virginia coun-try west of St. Paul as 2-8-8-2 No. 2181 leads a freight extra across the trestle that spans the Clinch River. Near here, the N&W interchanges freight with the Clinchfield Railroad. Photo-graphed June 25, 1953. At this time it was still impossible for the human mind to comprehend such trains as being powered by *anything* but steam-driven re-ciprocating power.

(both)N&W, VPI&SU

A few years later on August 21, 1959, again on a high trestle near St. Paul, on the N&W's Clinch Valley Line, no less than five of the huge Alco RS-11s power a train now that steam has almost gone from the N&W.

The Clinch Valley Train rounds a curve at colorfully named Pounding Mill, Virginia, in August 1954. Since the train operated as a "turn" with a 2:30 layover at Norton, the consist that day would be the same regardless of whether it was Train No. 5 or No. 6. Pacific No. 578 has charge of the run this August 1954 day.

Ed Crist Coll.

Canting gracefully through a superelevated "S" curve, GP-9s No. 722 and 750 carry an odd assortment of hoppers, box cars, tank cars, and gondolas near of Bluefield May 27, 1958.

(both) N&W, VPI&SU

An eastbound coal train behind five RS-11s (No. 369 in the lead), approaching Elkhorn Tunnel on the heavy grade that challenged eastbound coal movements, in February 1959. Note slide fence behind train. Fence detects any rocks that may have ambled on to the tracts and activates the block signals to prevent a wreck.

(Left) Alco RS-11 No. 321, followed by an RS-3 and two more RS-11s, make an interesting sight as they pull hard with eastbound coal at Big Four, West Virginia, about four miles east of Welch, on May 10 1956.

(Right) Two GP-9s and two RS-11s, alternately spliced, lug an eastbound coal drag through Maybeury, West Virginia, on the Elkhorn Grade, February 1, 1957.

(Below) Just east of Welch in June 1959, extra 2183 passes three Alco pushers waiting for extra 2199 (the last Y6b built), running right behind the 2183. This mix of motive power in West Virginia coal fields was an everyday sight as steam ran out its final hours.

(both) N&W, VPI&SU

47

Gene Huddleston

In Iaeger's smokey, gloomy Auville yard, it appears to be business as usual for steam—and indeed it will be thus another year. But Geep No. 791 peeking out from between the tenders of two of the steamers is a portent of what lies ahead for this gritty piece of West Virginia real estate.

Y-6a No. 2145 had spent many years hauling merchandise freight on the Shenandoah Division and later powering coal drags on the mainline east of Roanoke. But the year is 1959—the sunset of steam—and the powerful Mallet is running off the few remaining months of her life as a grimy mine shifter on the Dry Branch line. Here she's backing across the Tug Fork on the way into Iaeger yard.

(both)Gene Huddleston

A typical West Virginia coal tipple is in the background of GP-9 No. 872 and its two mates just east of Williamson, West Virginia on June 29, 1963.

Class-A 2-6-6-4 No. 1208 is taking its rated 190 cars from Williamson to Portsmouth. The train is along the Tug Fork near Kermit. The grade has indeed flattened out but the endless curves along the Tug make good use of the A's articulation and twelve drivers.

Gene Huddleston

Near Maybeury, West Virginia, on the Elkhorn Grade, five Alcos strain with Tidewater-bound coal on May 10, 1956. The hulking RS-11s had just been delivered to the N&W, having rolled out of the Schenectady shops in April of that year.

Williamson Engine Terminal

It has been said that the N&W dieselized without diesels because it standardized its principal motive power needs using a few highly developed standard steam locomotives that were maintained and serviced much as diesels were on other railroads. This ensured a much higher than ordinary utilization for N&W's mainstay locomotives. They were serviced in efficient, fast, modern terminals such as the one completed at Williamson, West Virginia, in 1946. When diesels arrived a decade later, these facilities were easily adapted to the new motive power operations.

N&W Photo, T. W. Dixon Coll.

The "Lubritorium," a long rectangular locomotive servicing building, was the key element in the modern N&W locomotive terminal, where engines were serviced and turned around for new assignments with a speed that amazed other railroads. Facilities such as these were easily converted to diesel servicing on the same type of turn-around rotation as the steam.

(Left) An exterior view of the Williamson engine service building shows A-class 2-6-6-4 No. 1232 emerging as another locomotive heads in the opposite direction.

(Below) An impressive night view of Williamson's engine service facilities, taken from atop the coal dock.

This diesel-era photo shows how easily the steam service facilities were adapted to the new motive power, leading some to say that the N&W had actually dieselized in overall locomotive service and utilization policies a decade before the diesels arrived.

(Above) J- and A-class locomotives populate the Williamson terminal, kept as clean as a model layout by N&W's proud employees.

(Below) A general view of Williamson shows office, roundhouse, water station, lubritorium, ash pits, and coaling station.

(both) N&W Photos. T. W. Dixon Coll.

RS-11 No. 398 heads up a westbound train ready to leave Williamson at 10:15 p.m. July 10, 1960.

Aubrey Wiley

Gene Huddleston

In a scene common at the time, a pair of Geeps, headed by No. 621, trundles 190 empty hoppers through Kermit, West Virginia, en route to Williamson, while Y6a-class 2-8-8-2 No. 2166, reduced to shifter status, occupied a siding at right as the steamer's crew ties up at a local beanery for lunch. Train orders await the drag's crew. Since 190 empties was about a normal load for the A-class 2-6-6-4s, it would appear that a pair of GP-9s was equivalent to an A. Hardly so, however. In this sort of service, where speed is not a necessity and the grade gentle, it was in all liklihood more economical to operate the diesel than one of the huge articulateds. But if that was a hotshot freight of comparable tonnage, at least one additional growler would have been needed to get the train from Portsmouth to Williamson in the same time as an A.

(*Left and below*) Leased Atlantic Coast Line E-7 (lettered N&W) leads the eastbound *Powhatan Arrow* into the two-level N&W/C&O station at Kenova, West Virginia, as C&O's manifest No. 93 rolls through westbound on the tracks below in October 1958 during the period that N&W leased ACL and RF&P E-units to immediately dieselize the passenger trains while waiting for delivery of passenger-equipped GP-9s.

(both) H. H. Harwood, Jr.

GP-9s 884 (*left*) and 863 (*right*) are rambling across the mighty Ohio River at Kenova in October 1959.

54

(both) N&W, VPI&SU

(Above) Class A No. 1218 (famous in the 1980s-90s as an excursion engine) attacks the short grade just east of the Kenova station headed west in February 1956.   *(Below)* Doubleheaded K2 and K2a 4-8-2s Nos. 123 and 133 *blast* out of Kenova eastbound in February 1956 with the *Cavalier*.

(both) H. H. Harwood, Jr.

Eastbound empty hoppers were not much load, and 190 of them were putting no great strain on GP-9s 794 and 799 at Ironton, Ohio. Note the loaded DT&I coke cars with built-up wooden sides. The DT&I line paralled the N&W through Ironton. Taken in Summer of 1958.

In the typically pancake-flat Ohio country around Haverhill on the Scioto Division, GP-9s Nos. 791 and 809 were adequate for muscling 190 empties from Portsmouth to Williamson. Photographed in 1957.

J-class No. 606 with the eastbound *Cavalier* crusing along the Ohio River near Haverhill, Ohio. The low hills in the background are in Kentucky.

(all) Gene Huddleston

56

Joe Schmitz

(Above) Steam still rules at Portsmouth, Ohio engine facility in July 1957.

(Below) Passenger Geeps Nos. 507, 501, and 500 lead the eastbound *Powhatan Arrow* through Portsmouth in June 1967. The dome car right behind the head-end cars was inherited from the Wabash in the 1964 merger.

Tom Dressler Photo; Howard W. Ameling Coll.

Gene Huddleston

(Above) S-1 Switcher backs up with a cut at the west end of Portsmouth yard in 1959. Note the built up tender coal bunker and water space sides. **(Below, left)** July 1957 view of the coaling station at Portsmouth with two steamers servicing. **(Below, right)** Back in 1962, Extra 354 west, with coal cars stretching as far as the eye can see, is at Haverhill, Ohio, between Portsmouth and Ironton. RS-11s Nos. 391 and 319 are assisting the 354.

(Left) Another load of "fuel satisfaction" is Columbus bound near Sargent's, Ohio.

(Right) Long nose (front on N&W) of GP-9 651.

K. L. Miller Coll.

(Below) A-class 2-6-6-4 No. 1202 with a light exhaust trailing back over the train indicating considerable speed, wheels manifest freight No. 85 on the straight and flat N&W west of Chillicothe, Ohio, in the mid-1950s.

(both) N&W, VPI&SU

Jawn Henry poses with J-class 4-8-4 No. 605 for N&W's official photographer soon after delivery of the monstrous new locomotive that N&W hoped would save coal-fired motive power on the road. The size of the steam-turbine is evident in this side-by-side portrait.

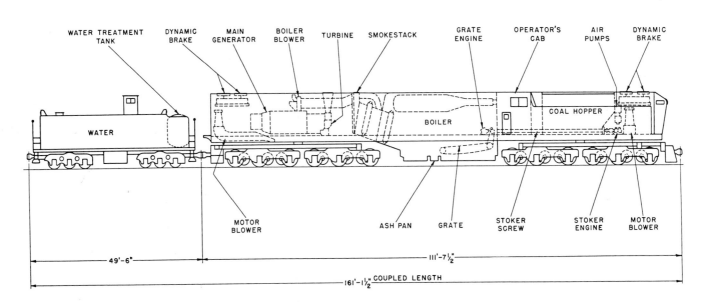

(both) N&W, VPI&SU

Official N&W publicity diagram shows the arrangement of major components of the *Jawn Henry*. Like the C&O's Steam-Turbine-Electric of 1948, the coal hopper was located in the nose. Unlike the C&O locomotives, a high-pressure water-tube boiler was located behind the control cab. The tender was for water only. The diagram's statistics indicated that the locomotive weighed 1,130,000 pounds, had 175,000 pounds of starting tractive effort, and 144,000 pounds of continuous tractive effort, and was rated at 4,500 horsepower.

Another N&W publicity photo shows *Jawn* in an impressive low angle view. The conservative, solid black steam-engine style paint scheme was in sharp contrast to the 1948 C&O Turbine-electric which was painted bright orange and silver!

The N&W dynamometer car was a common passenger behind *Jawn Henry's* drawbar immediately after its appearance on line since the N&W management was vitally interested in knowing the exact capabilities and efficiencies of the new technology.

At Shawsville, Virginia, *Jawn Henry* powers a merchandise train, followed again by the dynamometer car.

(all) N&W, VPI&SU

G. C. Corey Photo, H. H. Harwood Coll.

The date is August 1954 and *Jawn Henry* is westbound with hotshot freight No. 85 at Shawsville, Virginia during testing. Although *Jawn Henry* got a workout on the manifests, he pretty much ended up in pusher service—an ignominious ending for so special a locomotive. Men atop the coal bunker are monitoring performance and were almost a regular fixture.

Jawn moves an empty train, with dynamometer car, out of Bluefield yard soon after its arrival on the road.

E. P. Street photo; H. H. Harwood, Jr. Coll.

Here, in August 1954, *Jawn* is tackling Christiansburg Grade with a westbound freight. Note the laborers on top of the engine monitoring performance and coal consumption.